Foreword
by
Rev. Osbert Blankson Eduam
&
Apostle Theodore Quarcoopome

40 Wisdom Lessons on Prayer

From the life of Jesus Christ

Kojo Owusu-Ansah

ISBN: 978 - 9988 - 2 - 7474 - 0

Kojo Owusu-Ansah
P.O. Box BT 535
Tema
Tel: +233(0) 545 309 992
E-mail: kowusuansah@gmail.com
Twitter: @kojo_owusuansah
Instagram: Kojo_owusuansah
Facebook: www.facebook.com/kojo.owusuansah.7
Website: www.kojoowusuansah.org

Editing by Mrs. Samilia Eshun
Email: samiliad@yahoo.com
Mobile: +233 20 024 6954

Designed and Printed by
Kobina Eshun
Email: kobina.eshun@gmail.com
Mobile: +233 20 833 5437

Other books by the author:
The Right Foundation
Dimensions of Grace
Consider the Lilies
The Touch of Jesus

DEDICATION

To my Father Christian Yaw Owusu-Ansah.

To the Prayer Force of Life International Church - Faith Chapel. Thank you for giving me the opportunity to serve the church through prayer. May the LORD bless and establish you all.

To my mentor and friend Evans Darko-Mensah. You make Christianity so pleasant to desire every day. You always bring out the GOOD in the news for all your listeners. Thank you for your advice and guidance through the scriptures.

To Rev. Eric and Mrs. MargareteTenkorang. Thank you for giving me a gift of destiny. I still remember your gift. God richly bless you.

To my friend Charles Amanor. You are more than a brother to me. Thank you for being there for me always.

Contents

ACKNOWLEDGEMENT

My utmost gratitude goes to the Most High God for His grace to come out with yet another book and I am indebted also to a host of people whose influence and prayers have helped me come this far.

To the General Overseer of Life International Church Bishop Gor-don Kisseih and wife Apostle Mrs. Esther Kisseih, I'm grateful to God for your lives and your ministry through which I gained my foundation in Christ.

To my wonderful parents, family and siblings: Mr. & Mrs. Apke, Owusu-Ansah family, Ackon family, Mrs. Comfort Baidoo, Yaw Kesse, Sarah, Ama, Setor, Ato and Enyo you are always a part of me.

To Apostle Theodore Quarcoopome and wife Pastor Mrs. Sefenya Quarcoopome, Rev. Jacob Zotbah, Pastor Augustine Owusu Asare and the entire family of Life International Church (L.I.C) - Faith Chapel, God richly bless you for your love and encouragement.

To the youth executives of L.I.C Faith Chapel, I am indebted for the love and dedication in supporting me in my leadership role as the Youth President.

To Mr. Emmanuel and wife Samilia Eshun, thanks for the great editorial work, graphics and printing.

Many thanks also go to all those who supported with their presence and presents during my first and second book launches. You make writing exciting and hopeful. God richly bless you.

FOREWORD
BY
REV. OSBERT BLANKSON EDUAM

Prayer is an integral part of our Spiritual walk with God, yet little attention and recognition is given to it by many. Prayer is a universal code of communication used in hundreds of religions and spiritual sects all over the world.

In this book, Kojo has taken on the subject of Prayer and has explored a framework of lessons and principles that are readily available and easily understood for practitioners.

There are several aspects of the book I found exceptionally useful and relevant in building a solidified prayer life.

First and foremost, aside the core subject of prayer, this book intends to unearth the focus of result oriented prayer through the phases of execution, which leads to potent spiritual and physical benefit. Secondly, it has highlighted real life examples to illustrate the lesson, principle and subject factors to consider when apply-ing the lessons and principles.

It finally makes known to the reader that, sensitivity to the word of God and a willingness to change prayer strategies, but not objectives, are critical when it comes to communing with our Creator. The biblical references used to expatiate the various lessons, give the reader clear and precise ideas that place relevance on the subject or lesson being dissected. Furthermore this book also places a strong attachment to God, making him the entire source of power and man, the sole connecting figure to God for answers.

It is also clear that the application of these 40 wisdom lesson positions an individual in directing prayers to acquire significant results within a time frame of expectancy. In the book, the writer shares principles or lessons that intend to teach Christians to know the importance of prayer in the light of changing lives, connecting man to the divinity of God, the anointing opportunities prayer uncovers, the success prayer brings, and the obstacles prayer re-moves amongst others.

Having been involved in prayer as a Minister of the gospel of our lord Jesus Christ for decades now, I strongly recommend this book to all who want to understand the subject of prayer for benefits found only in the word of God.

Rev. Osbert Blankson Eduam
Head Pastor of Life Empowerment Chapel,
Sakomono, Accra, Ghana

Board of Director WEL GROUP LLC

FOREWORD
BY
APOSTLE THEODORE QUARCOOPOME

Prayer has been, and will continue to be the greatest and richest resource for the Christian life and ministry. Indeed many success-es in life and ministry have been the result of wholehearted prayer in conjunction with wisdom resulting from prayerful meditation on the Word of God. Prayer continues to be the key factor in reviv-al, salvation of souls and in solving complex life challenges.

This book '40 Wisdom Lessons on Prayer – From The Life of Je-sus Christ' by Kojo Owusu-Ansah is intended to bring out lessons from the prayer lifestyle and teachings of Jesus Christ who ex-perienced great depths in prayer and did great exploits through prayer while on earth. Each chapter of the book reveals a particu-lar lesson to be learnt from Jesus who is the greatest example of a person who prayed earnestly and agonizingly such that his sweat was like great drops of blood falling down to the ground (Luke 22: 44).

Knowing how to pray and actually praying is so important that E. M. Bounds is quoted as saying that 'I would rather teach a man how to pray than to preach many sermons'. Praying is neither meant to be a ritual nor is it meant to be done on trial and error basis but rather praying is meant to be effective (achieving desired results) and must be based on principles.

It is expected that the lessons drawn from the prayer life and teach-ings of Jesus Christ Himself as outlined in this book will so inform and illuminate you to the extent that you will begin or continue in incessant, instant, consistent and persistent prayer to transform you and cause you to achieve desired results in your private and public life, in your family, ministry and career as well as nationally and internationally. This is because God rules the world through the passionate praying of His saints.

This book is written in a simple, concise, precise and easy to understand form. It is, therefore, suitable for all age groups. I, hereby, strongly recommend this book for all those who desire to see their faith established, their lives and ministries become enriched through effective praying and their prayer making impact on peo-ple, issues and events in this generation and in the generations to come.

Apostle Theodore Quarcoopome
Senior Pastor
Life International Church
Faith Chapel, Community 5, Tema

INTRODUCTION

Prayer is the soul's sincere desire,
Uttered or unexpressed,
The motion of a hidden fire
That trembles in the breast.

Prayer is the burden of a sigh,
The falling of a tear,
The upward glancing of an eye
When none but God is near.

Prayer is the simplest form of speech
That infant lips can try;
Prayer is the sublimest strains that reach
The majesty on high.

Prayer is the contrite sinner's voice
Returning from his ways,
While angels in their songs rejoice,
And cry: Behold, he prays!

Prayer is the Christian's vital breath,
The Christian's native air,
His watchword at the gates of death;
He enters heaven with prayer.

O Thou by whom we come to God, The
Life, the Truth, the Way! The path of
prayer Thyself hast trod; Lord! Teach us
how to pray.[1]

---

1   James Montgomery, "Prayer is the Soul's Sincere Desire." 1818.

Prayer is a communication with God based on His Word in the name of Jesus. Prayer is the greatest need of everyone who would be saved and those who are saved because it takes one to believe and pray to be saved. The believer is also admonished to pray without ceasing.

Many are those who are frustrated about prayer because they pray and don't seem to get any answers. It is either they don't pray right or don't know how to receive from God. At times, we just do the talking and refuse to allow God to speak to us in our prayers. We forget that prayer is communication. Communication is the exchange of information. There has to be someone speaking, listening, receiving and/or replying.

Some also think prayer is not in the equation of success but in the equation of revelation. That is true but not the full truth. Prayer serves a lot of purposes and is in every equation of life. An atheist doesn't pray but he appears to be successful. People in other religions necessarily do not pray to our God but they also appear to be successful and wealthy. But I assure you that they have no power over the devil that attacks them. The devil can devour them anytime, any day, anywhere. That's why the believer in the Lord has an upper hand. This is because he can engage prayer in the equation of godly success and enjoy the blessings of God without sorrow.

It is vital to understand prayer and how it works in order to enjoy its maximum benefits. There are various forms of prayer and these include prayer of agreement, prayer of petition, prayer of commitment, prayer of praise, worship and thanksgiving, prayer of faith, prayer of consecration and prayer of supplication.

The focus of this book is not to show you how to pray nor explain the various forms of prayer to you but to expound on what prayer stands for and what it can do. The lessons shared here can change your attitude to prayer, stir you up for a life of prayer and impact your life positively forever.

I think it will also be good to explain briefly how to pray, the various kinds of prayer and how to receive answers to your prayers to enable you take maximum advantage of all the lessons shared about prayer in this book.

The disciples asked Jesus to teach them how to pray and our Lord Jesus taught them to pray in what is popularly called 'the Lord's Prayer'. The Lord's Prayer is deeper than just what we know to be what Jesus said according to Matthew 6:9-13 (NKJV):

In this manner, therefore, pray:

Our Father in heaven,
Hallowed be Your name.
Your kingdom come.
Your will be done
On earth as *it is* in heaven.
Give us this day our daily bread.
And forgive us our debts,
As we forgive our debtors.
And do not lead us into temptation, But deliver us from the evil one. For Yours is the kingdom and the power and the glory forever. Amen.

Each sentence stands for a topic we can use to pray. When I want to pray for long hours this is the same strategy I mostly use:

Our Father in heaven, Hallowed be Your name: Jesus made us to understand that God is our Father. We are not praying to someone we don't know or an entity somewhere up there. God is our Father meaning anyone who is a believer is also our brother and sister since we all have the same Father. To hallow the name of the Lord is to worship, praise and thank him for who he is and for all he has done.

Your kingdom come: The kingdom of God is about his righteousness, peace and joy in the Holy Spirit (Romans 14:17). Pray for God's righteousness, peace and joy to gain expression in your life, family, church and nation. It takes righteousness to exalt a nation (Proverbs 14:34). Most people pray for the peace of their nation but if wicked people are ruling then there will be no peace because scripture says, "There is no peace," says the Lord "for the wicked"(Isaiah 48:22). It takes righteousness to have peace. When righteousness is present, peace and joy are evident.

Your will be done on earth as it is in heaven: The will of God is good, pleasing and perfect (Romans 12:2). Here you must pray for God's will to be done in your life concerning any desires you have in your heart be it a life partner, a course to study, a travel-ling appointment among many others.

Give us this day our daily bread: This is to ask God for your daily needs or provisions. Our Father provides for our needs and it will be good to ask him. Jesus said you do not have because you do not ask. Ask and you will receive and your joy will be full (John 16:24). By this prayer also you can ask our Father to give you a scripture, which is your spiritual food to meditate on throughout the day.

And forgive us our debts, as we forgive our debtors: When Jesus was teaching this prayer, he had not shed his blood to cleanse the sins of mankind. Now Jesus has shed his blood and there is forgiveness of sin in his blood (Hebrews 9:22). Sin is a nature and if you are in Christ that nature has been replaced with his free gift of righteousness (2 Corinthians 5:21). I believe by this prayer you should thank our Father for the forgiveness we have in Jesus Christ and ask for the grace to forgive anyone who has hurt you or will hurt you in the future.

And do not lead us into temptation, but deliver us from the evil one: By this prayer you ask our Father for his guidance in all you are doing and his deliverance from evil just as he has promised us in his Word (Psalm 91).

For yours is the kingdom and the power and the glory forever: Here you thank our Father for hearing your prayers. You can as well magnify him because to Him is the kingdom, power and glo-ry now and forever. Amen.

To receive answers to your prayers is not dependent on our Father but you. Jesus said something remarkable here, "Therefore I say to you, whatever things you ask when you pray, believe that you receive them, and you will have them (Mark 11:24)." As long as you are praying according to the will of God he hears and answers you but if you doubt then according to what Jesus said you will not have them.

The important thing here is to believe God has heard and answered. The best thing to do between the time God answers and when you have the answers with you is to give thanks to God. Thanksgiving shows your appreciation to God for answering you. It keeps you in Faith to receive what you have asked in prayer. By this knowledge we can proceed to our Prayer Lessons.

Matthew 6:9

After this manner therefore pray ye: Our Fa
- ther which art in Heaven, Hallowed be thy
name.

1

PRAYER CAN BE TAUGHT

In the book of Matthew, Jesus taught the multitude on the moun-tain on a number of subjects ranging from salt and light, law, anger, lust, divorce, prayer amongst many others. In the book of Luke Chapter 11, one of Jesus' disciples approached him after he had finished praying and he said to him, "Lord, teach us to pray, just as John taught his disciples." (Luke 11:1)

The model of what has been known as the Lord's Prayer is what I expounded on in the introduction of this book. Prayer is very vital to the survival of mankind and we need not go about it with emp-ty heads as if everyone can just get up and pray. Many Christians are frustrated when it comes to prayer. The last thing they want to hear is for them to be told of another prayer meeting. They are so frustrated that they see prayer as a waste of time because they seem not to lay their hands on anything prayer has brought to them or caused them to achieve.

What is very vital to life cannot be overlooked or underestimat-ed. Prayer should not be engaged in by common sense or you get a common sense result. Prayer is work and every work requires training to maximise the resources of the organisation.

The Word of God, the Holy Spirit, your time, mind, strength, breath, voice and entire being are some of the resources needed for prayer. One must know how to engage each and every part of it very well to enjoy the benefits of prayer.

Jesus took his time to teach his disciples how to pray. Parents must take their time to teach their children how to pray. Pastors must take their time to teach their congregation how to pray. Every individual must take his or her time to learn how to pray and we must ask the Holy Spirit to teach us how to pray because every situation and the kind of prayer required or needed to handle it.

It will take the wisdom of God to discern and know the right prayer to use for any given situation. It is therefore important for one to really learn how to pray.

John 16:24
Until now you have asked nothing in My
name. Ask, and you will receive, that your
joy may be full.

2

PRAYER IS IN THE NAME OF JESUS

Our communication to God is in the name of Jesus. God our Father has no obligation to hear and answer the prayers of anyone except it comes to him in the name of Jesus and in accor-dance to His will and purpose. Prayer for believers is in the name of Jesus because Jesus himself said we should ask in his name. "Until now you have asked nothing in my name. Ask, and you will receive, that your joy may be full" (John 16:24).

Also, Jesus satisfied the wrath of God fully and He is the Beloved son of God in whom He is well pleased. Once we come to God in the name of Jesus, we are accepted in the Beloved. "Blessed be the God and Father of our Lord Jesus Christ, who has blessed us with every spiritual blessing in the heavenly places in Christ, just as He chose us in Him before the foundation of the world, that we should be holy and without blame before Him in love, having predestined us to adoption as sons by Jesus Christ to Himself, according to the good pleasure of His will, to the praise of the glory of His grace, by which He made us accepted in the Beloved." (Ephesians 1:3-6).

In addition, when we pray in the name of Jesus we are telling God we are here on the basis of what Jesus has done for us. Jesus paid the full penalty for our sins on the cross and we are telling God to look at Jesus and answer our prayers. "For Christ also suffered once for sins, the just for the unjust, that He might bring us to

God, being put to death in the flesh but made alive by the Spirit" (1 Peter 3:18).

Jesus is also our High Priest and Advocate. When we pray in His name it is like he is offering our prayers to God for us since He lives forever to make intercession for us. "Therefore He is also able to save to the uttermost those who come to God through Him, since He always lives to make intercession for them" (Hebrews 7:25).

Beloved, the name of Jesus is higher and above every other name. At the mention of that name every knee bows of things in heav-en on earth and under the earth. Enjoy the privilege of using the name of Jesus in your prayers always.

James 4:8

Draw near to God and He will draw near to you. Cleanse your hands, you sinners; and purify your hearts, you double-minded.

3

PRAYER STRENGTHENS OUR RELATIONSHIP WITH GOD

The more you pray the more you get to know God and the greater your prayer results will be. God is available for all his children but those who pray get his attention and are able to draw close to him. When you draw close to God, you get the oppor-tunity to hear his majestic voice that leads to all profiting in life (Isaiah 48:17).

Jesus could not do anything on his own but as he heard from God he was able to judge and his judgement was just because He sought not his own will but the will of the Father. As we go through life we make a lot of decisions or judgements on our next line of action. But through prayer God is able to lead us to make the right judgements.

Jesus who by himself is the Word of God spent time in prayer. He prayed for long hours and also prayed for short periods. Between his prayer times were miracles. He was so close to the Father through prayers that his disciples saw it and requested he taught them to pray. Every relationship thrives on communication. Most often, God speaks to us through his word and in prayer and our way of speaking to him is through prayer.

To build a strong relationship with God, we must invest more time in prayer just as Jesus did. For those who know their God will be great and they shall do exploits in the name of Jesus (Daniel 11:32).

Luke 9:29
As He prayed, the appearance of His face
was altered, and His robe became white
and glistening.

4

PRAYER CHANGES YOU

Great and lasting destinies are built on prayer. Jesus went to the mountain to pray and as He prayed the appearance of His face transformed and His clothes became dazzling white. Every lasting transformation comes about through prayer. Jesus' counte-nance would not have changed if He had not spent time in prayer. Any situation in your life can be changed through prayer.

In the Bible, certain individuals changed their lives by prayer. The life of Jacob, Jabez, Hannah and many others were transformed through prayer. Today, prayer can change your situation. Jacob's name was changed through prayer. Prayer has the potency to avert, overturn, nullify and overrule problems in your life.

Blind Bartimaeus had his story changed by calling on Jesus (Matthew 10:46-52). The leprous man received his healing by calling on Jesus (Matthew 8:1-4). Beloved, when you call on Jesus all things are possible. No condition is permanent in your life. That sickness will not kill you. That debt can be cancelled. Your promotion and progress will come speedily by prayer.

By prayer any garment of shame can be changed to a garment of praise. Any mourning can be changed into dancing. Any ashes can be changed into beauty. Any robe of shame and disgrace can be changed into a white and glistening robe. Any sickness can be changed into health. Any curse can be changed into a blessing.

Any defeat can be changed into victory. Any fear can be changed into boldness. I see your change coming by prayer in Jesus name. You are blessed!

Matthew 18:18-19

Assuredly, I say to you, whatever you bind on earth will be bound in heaven, and what-ever you loose on earth will be loosed in heaven. Again I say to you that if two of you agree on earth concerning anything that they ask, it will be done for them by My Father in heaven.

5

PRAYER IS A LAW

Merriam-Webster dictionary defines law as the whole system or set of rules made by the government of a town, state, country, etc. Prayer is a law made by God. God is the sovereign King of his kingdom and he has set a rule that unless you pray to him (or others pray to him for you) there is no way he can inter-vene in your situation. God does not respond to the cries of people but the prayers of the saints. God has given man the authority to rule on earth. He will not in any way intervene in this ruler-ship unless we allow him. Whatever you choose to allow on earth is what will be allowed in heaven and whatever you choose to dis-allow on earth will be disallowed in heaven (Matthew 18:18-19).

Heaven is waiting for your commands here on earth to back them. God himself has set this rule in the world He has created to bring about orderliness. The angels of the Lord heed to the voice of his word (Psalm 103:20). Nothing moves them except the word of God. This order is put in place by God.

It's so worrying how people will be adamant to the way things are happening and later blame God. God may not even move a finger if man refuses to pray about anything. Complaining and crying doesn't solve anything. It is prayer that causes God to intervene. Psalm 115:16 says, "The heaven, even the heavens, are the Lord's; But the earth He has given to the children of men." It is therefore the responsibility of man to have dominion on earth but to overcome Satan and his cohorts we also need the intervention of God and that happens when one prays.

Jesus said, "Assuredly, I say to you, whatever you bind on earth will be bound in heaven, and whatever you loose on earth will be loosed in heaven. Again I say to you that if two of you agree on earth concerning anything that they ask, it will be done for them by My Father in heaven" (Matthew 18:18-19). This is a rule or a law set in place by Jesus. The demands of this law will answer to you any day, anytime, anywhere.

Zechariah 12:10

And I will pour on the house of David and on
the inhabitants of Jerusalem the Spirit of
grace and supplication

6

PRAYER IS A SPIRIT AND IT NEVER DIES

To die is to come to an end. It is to be invalid after a period of time or to expire but prayer never expires or dies. Prayer is a spirit and spirits don't die. If prayers don't die then it's a good rea-son to engage in more prayers. Jesus said, the words that I speak to you are spirit and life. If we engage the Word of God which is spirit in prayer then we are engaged in a serious spiritual activity.

The Spirit of prayer and the Spirit of the Word will always birth a miracle. When we sleep, travel or engage in any activity, we pray for God's protection, guidance, and blessings. We believe these prayers will work out because they never expire or die. You pray and sleep knowing God will keep watch over you. That prayer will sustain you even whiles you are still asleep. This shows that prayer never dies or expires as long as what you believe God for hasn't come to pass yet. Then, that prayer is still at work, never cancel such prayer because they will work for you.

The prayer for salvation is what will secure your place in heaven when you are gone. Prayer deals with matters beyond the grave. You can die but your prayers never die. The only investment that will profit all generations to come is prayer because it does not expire and every generation that comes stands the chance of ben-efiting from its impact. The prayers of Jesus in John 17 were for all who will believe in him and that prayer is still speaking today after over 2000 years when he ascended to heaven. E.M. Bounds said, "Prayer is the only thing that takes hold of eternity and mat-ters beyond the grave."

Do not stop praying. Every prayer time should be an opportunity for investing in the future. Your tomorrow blessings are your prayers today because prayer never dies.

Luke 18:1

Then He spoke a parable to them, that men
always ought to pray and not lose heart

7

PRAYER MAKES YOU SUCCESSFUL

Failure to pray is failure in all of life and the vice versa is also true. Prayer makes you successful in this life. In every endeav-our it takes prayer to succeed. There are times the experts fail and experience doesn't yield any results. Peter and his colleagues toiled all night and caught nothing that night. They had been in the fishing business for so many years but that didn't guarantee a catch. As soon as they spoke to Jesus he told them to cast the net on the right side and they caught many fish (John 21:1-6).

You can also speak to Jesus about that business, marriage, education, children, etc., and he will show you the right side that will make you successful. Only pray to him and your success is assured.

The children of Israel were about to be annihilated by the devising schemes of Haman but by fasting and prayers, the decree went in their favour and their enemies were killed instead. I see that court case turning to your favour by reason of your prayer. Anything making you toil for nothing is turning in your favour. You are coming out victorious. Your prayers are working for you.

All the questions of life have answers and how to locate the answers is by prayer. It is even through prayer that your eyes are opened to behold wondrous truth out of the Word of God (Psalm 119:18). The letter kills but the Spirit gives life. Engaging the word of God to secure answers has its foundation in prayer. Everyone can read the Word of God but it takes prayer to have insight, revelation and spiritual understanding to solve the questions of life. (Ephesians 1:17-18). Prayer therefore serves as the bedrock upon which successful destinies are built.

Mark 11:23

For assuredly, I say to you, whoever says to
this mountain, 'Be removed and be cast into
the sea,' and does not doubt in his heart,
but believes that those things he says will
be done, he will have whatever he says.

8

PRAYER REMOVES IMPOSSIBLE OBSTACLES

That which seems to be a barrier and sets the limits for each one of us can be annulled by prayer. Prayer is one thing that opposes the oppressor, sets a new standard and destroys any impediment.

Jesus said to the disciples that they can say to this mountain (obstacle), "be removed and be cast into the sea" and by their faith it will be done. Prayer moves mountains that have become obstacles out of your way. Anything that hinders your progress is an obsta-cle.

They were hindered by their leprosy but this ten member associa-tion of lepers decided to call on the Lord Jesus to heal them. Hin-dered by his sight, reduced to a beggar and unable to carry out his full potential, blind Bartimaeus defied the odds and cried out the more to Jesus son of David to open his eyes.

Their smooth sailing or progress in life was intercepted by a storm. The disciples called on Jesus to save them. They brought a demon oppressed man who was unable to speak and Jesus healed him. The disciples were being hindered in their assignment after the ascension of Jesus, they cried out to God and that settled it.

If you can also call on God today, that sickness which seems impossible to go will leave. The unawarded contract will be awarded to you. That which has caused you shame and for that matter you can't go to public gathering will be removed in Jesus name.

Whatever project you have began will be completed in Jesus name. Nothing will hinder you anymore. Your hands have laid the foun-dation and by your hands you shall finish. Then you will know that the Lord of hosts is greater than any obstacle.

Revelation 1:5-6

…and from Jesus Christ, the faithful witness, the
firstborn from the dead, and the ruler over the
kings of the earth. To Him who loved
us and washed us from our sins in His own
blood, and has made us kings and priests to
His God and Father, to Him be glory and dominion forever and ever. Amen.

9

PRAYER STIRS THE KINGLY AND PRIESTLY ANOINTING

In the Old Testament it was only the king and the priest who were anointed to serve in their respective roles. Samuel anointed Saul to become the first King of Israel and scripture says the Spirit of God rested on Saul and he began to prophesy. The anointing that came upon him symbolised authority and power in the new role he was to play. So Solomon in the book of Ecclesiastes said, "where the word of a king is, there is power…" The priests were also anointed to serve in their respective positions in the temple of God. The anointing of the priest symbolised holiness, consecra-tion and intercession. Before they ministered unto God they were to consecrate themselves or else they will die and they interceded for the entire nation of Israel.

Jesus Christ came to save and redeem us from sins. Not only did he do that, but has also made us kings and priests unto God. What this means is everyone who is in Christ Jesus is automatically a king and a priest. What only some few selected people enjoyed in the Old Testament is now enjoyed by all believers all over the world. Peter also confirmed this by saying, "we are a chosen gen-eration, a royal priesthood, an holy nation, a peculiar people; that ye show forth the praises of him who hath called you out of dark-ness into his marvellous light" (1 Peter 2:9).

To be a king means your words carry power and authority. To be a priest means you have to live a life of holiness and consecration.

You can as well intercede without struggle for others.

These anointings we have are in our spirit. It takes prayer to stir them up for one to enjoy their maximum benefits. Prayer stirs the kingly anointing for your words to carry power and authority. Scripture says you shall decree a thing and it shall be established for you (Job 22:28). The kingly unction makes it possible for your words to be established. You can command sicknesses to leave and they will leave. You can call things that are dead to come back to life and it will happen for you. Your words become extraordi-nary so you must be careful about the things you say.

Prayer enables you to live a life of purity, consecration and gives you the grace to intercede for others. Stir up these anointing of Jesus in you now and enjoy all its benefits to the glory of God.

Matthew 14:19

Then He commanded the multitudes to sit down on the grass. And He took the five loaves and the two fish, and looking up to heaven, he blessed and broke and gave the loaves to the disciples; and the disciples gave

to the multitudes.

10

PRAYER OPENS THE HEAVENS

Open heavens is having the opportunity to access heavenly blessings. It is getting only what the heavens can provide. It is living the heavenly life here on earth and it is prayer that makes all these possible.

Jesus ministered to thousands of people and he decided to feed them because he realised they were hungry and might faint along on their way home. When he took the five loaves of bread and two fish, the first thing scripture says he did was **"blessed"** before he broke and gave.

The thanksgiving or blessings he rendered to God before breaking the bread was a prayer to God. In the story of Lazarus also he gave thanks to God before he commanded Lazarus to come forth. Je-sus' connection to God always opened the heavens for the super-natural to take place. The heavens belong to God (Psalm 115:16) and they are full of the supernatural. Anytime you want to have a touch of the supernatural in your life, the first key is prayer.

Elijah was a man like you and I but by prayer this man was able to shut and open the heavens. It rained in Israel by his terms and conditions. Every man of prayer is in control of affairs. Just as the heavens are higher than the earth so things from above are above all earthly things. Prayer will cause you to be above situations and circumstances.

Ephesians 1:17-18

That the God of our Lord Jesus Christ, the Father of glory, may give to you the spirit of wisdom and revelation in the knowledge of Him, the eyes of your understanding being enlightened; that you may know what is the hope of His calling, what are the riches of the glory of His inheritance in the saints.

11

PRAYER IS A MEDIUM OF DIVINE REVELATION

God shows himself to the one who prays. Insight, understand-ing and wisdom are mostly encountered through prayer.
Paul had to pray for the church of Ephesus that God gives them spiritual wisdom and understanding in the knowledge of him. For one to know Jesus, it takes divine revelation encountered through prayer and that is exactly what Paul did for the church in Ephesus.

In the case of Daniel, he was faced with a difficult situation that he didn't know where to turn to but God. He prayed his heart out to God concerning a dream that King Nebuchadnezzar had that he could not remember. However, he wanted someone to tell him the dream and interpret it to him. This was impossible to say but by prayer God revealed the dream to Daniel and showed him the interpretation of it (Daniel 2:17-23). God is still in the business of revealing hidden secrets to his people who pray to him. He re-veals deeds and hidden things and knows what is in the darkness.

Many are those who have encountered the Lord in prayer, re-ceived great business ideas, solved complex issues and discovered hidden treasures through prayer. Through prayer, God will reveal your wife or husband to you, he will show you your career or the right business plan to take, he will show you which land to buy or even where to locate your business or family. Wisdom was speak-ing in Proverbs and she said, "cry out for insight and understand-ing" (Proverbs 2:3).

Isaiah 40:31

But those who wait on the Lord shall renew
their strength; They shall mount up with
wings like eagles, They shall run and not
be weary, They shall walk and not faint.

12

PRAYER PRODUCES STRENGTH

Prayer gives strength to the weak. The dictionary defines strength as the emotional or mental qualities necessary in dealing with situations or events that are distressing or difficult.

There are times one goes through difficult situations and the only strength needed is the one the Spirit provides through prayer. Prayer builds the inner man to stand against any distressing or difficult situations. Scripture says build up yourself in your most holy faith praying in the language of the spirit (Jude 1:20).

When Jesus was about to be betrayed and crucified, he found strength in prayer. He went to the garden of Gethsemane and prayed to the Father that if it be His will let this cup pass over me (Matthew 26:39). The will of God for his life was to strengthen him for the task ahead. The Father empowered him to endure the cross despising the shame for the joy that was set before him.

The same will be true of our lives if we humble ourselves in prayer and seek his will in any difficult situation. He said even if you pass through the water He will be with you and when you walk through the fire He will be with you and you will not be burned (Isaiah 43:2). God has a way of preparing his children. We need not be frightened in difficult times because it is God who sets the times and seasons for our lives. In all things give thanks and the God of all glory will empower and strengthen you through the trying times.

Strength is very important for endurance. When the fire, wind, water and the storms of life come against you, it will only take the grace of God through the strength He provides to stand in such times.

The Holy Spirit bears his fruit in our lives by grace and prayer stirs the Spirit in our lives. Prayer stirs the Spirit in us and helps the gifts of the Spirit in us to come alive and active. Most of the time all we need is the character to stand in difficult times. Prayer brings strength of character to stand because after all we are re-quired by the Word to stand (Ephesians 6:13).

Matthew 26:53

Or do you think that I cannot now pray to
My Father, and He will provide Me with
more than twelve legions of angels?

13

PRAYERS GO EVERYWHERE

Prayer goes everywhere and lays its hand on anything. There is nowhere in the entire universe that prayers cannot en-ter. When Jesus was attacked and his disciples wanted to fight he said to them I can ask the Father and he will send down legions of angels to fight on my behalf. Prayer can enter everywhere. It can enter our homes, schools, government, markets, hospitals, malls and anywhere we desire.

Prayer has no limits and no one can underestimate its effect. Let your prayer go to places today. Let your prayer travel to nations to cause a move and a revival of the Holy Spirit. Let your prayer enter into the hospitals to bring healing and deliverance to weary souls. Let your prayer enter the government system to bring peace, godliness, righteousness, honour and dignity. Let your prayer enter war torn countries to bring about peace and order. Let your prayer travel today and see the power of God at work miles from where you are.

No place in the entire universe is immune to prayer. Even the elements are subject to the decrees of men. Joshua had to command the sun to stand still over Gibeon and the moon in the valley of Aijalon and these elements obeyed (Joshua 10:13). There are no boundaries when it comes to prayer, it goes everywhere.

Acts 4:31

And when they had prayed, the place where they were assembled together was shaken; and they were filled with the Holy Spirit, and they spoke the word of God with boldness.

14

PRAYER QUALIFIES THE MISSIONARY

Prayer is the primary qualifier of any missionary. Every missionary requires prayer to make it on the mission field. Paul always requested for the prayers of the saints on the mission field. At one time he asked the Thessalonian church to pray for them, that the word of God may run swiftly and be glorified, and that they may be delivered from unreasonable and wicked men; for not all have faith (2 Thessalonians 3:1-2). There are evil men every-where and it takes prayer to shield us from all their evil schemes.

Redeeming the souls of sinful men requires one to live the life of righteousness. The redeemer has to be distinct from the sinner and prayer makes that life of righteousness possible for the missionary for sinners to look to him as a true witness of the glorified Jesus Christ.

Missionary work without prayer is like playing among wolves unknowingly. It is such an important assignment that one needs not lose sight of it. Prayer keeps the vision alive and makes it fresh always. It enables power to rescue sinners, transform them and make them prayer champs as well.

The god of this world has blinded the minds of those who do not believe lest the light of the gospel of the glory of Christ, who is the image of God, should shine on them (2 Corinthians 4:4). Prayer removes any blindfolding for the light of the gospel to shine on all those who are perishing to come to the saving knowledge of Jesus.

Prayer was the bedrock of the missionary work of Jesus. His constant communion with the Father enabled him to judge rightly and obey the will of the Father even to the cross. Apostle Paul, a great missionary boasted of his much prayer than all the saints (1 Corinthians 14:18). Indeed, prayer qualifies one for missionary work.

Isaiah 59:1-2

Behold, the LORD'S hand is not shortened, that
it cannot save; Nor his ear heavy That it cannot
hear. But your iniquities have separat-ed you
from your God; And your sins have hidden His
face from you, So that he will not

hear.

15

PRAYER MOVES GOD'S HAND

Prayer moves the hand of God to bring deliverance down. The hand of God stands for God's power, strength and his ability to act on behalf of his children. Prayer is a good ground to see the hand of God at work in our lives.

The hand of God is able to bring goodness into your life (Ezra 8:18). The hand of God is able to create something for you and also bring creativity in your life (Psalm 119:73). The hand of God is able to satisfy your every desire (Psalm 145:16). The hand of God is able to come upon you and cause you to overtake in life (1 Kings 18:45-46). The hand of God is able to keep and deliver you from evil (John 10:28-29). The hand of God is able to uphold you (Isaiah 41:10).

Jesus (who is God) when He walked the face of the earth touched with His hand to bring miracle, deliverance, life, restoration, wholeness, healing, etc. to the people He touched. For instance, the woman who was bent over for eighteen years received the touch of Jesus. When Jesus saw her, he called her over and said to her, "Woman you are freed from your disability" And he laid His hands on her, and immediately she was made straight and she glorified God (Luke 13:12-13). Jesus spoke the word and touched her to make her whole.

Today, Jesus is not here physically to touch with His hand, but He has left us with his word and the Holy Spirit who is with us and also lives in us. Whenever we speak His word to any situation in His name He moves by His Spirit to change the situation. His power, strength and ability are made manifest when we use the word of God effectively in prayer.

John 10:27
My sheep hear my voice, and I know them,
and they follow me

16

PRAYER MAKES GREAT LEADERS

The leading of the LORD makes great leaders. Prayer ushers you into the realm to hear and discern his leading in order to follow and come out great and victorious. Leaders come and lead-ers go but the leader who prays makes an impression in the lives of the people he leads.

Leaders are known for the words they speak. Jesus said, "the words I speak are spirit and they are life" (John 6:63). One key thing followers use to remember their leaders are the words they speak whiles they are in office. That is why God has even exalted his word above his name (Psalm 138:2). Also, until heaven and earth pass away not a single word of his will fail (Mark 13:31). Words are powerful and prayer backs the words of a leader with power.

Leaders are noted for their character. Character attracts people, it determines how strong or weak you are, it shows how far you can go in life, it serves as your brand to market you wherever you go and in ministry it serves as collateral. The Holy Spirit in us pro-duces his character of love, joy, peace, patience, kindness, good-ness, faithfulness, gentleness and self-control (Galatians 5:22-23). Being conscious of this truth enables you to take advantage of it through prayer and that will make you a Christ-like believer and a true leader.

Leaders are people who serve. One form of service is to intercede for the people you are leading. Jesus interceded for Peter (Luke 22:32) and his disciples whiles on earth. He is also able to save those who come to God through Him, since he always lives to make intercession for them (Hebrews 7:25). If our Lord Jesus is still serving us by interceding for us, then we can easily emulate this example to intercede for those who are following us.

Leaders have vision and prayer gives clarity to the vision God gives. In the garden of Gethsemane Jesus prayed for the will of God to be done in his life. The vision of going to the cross was not an easy task but by prayers and supplications with strong crying and tears unto him who was able to save him from death, and was heard in that he feared (Hebrews 5:7). He was able to overcome.

Leadership is more than a position, it is more than just a responsibility, it is more than age, it is more than a certificate and it is more than a skill. It takes the grace of God to be a great and an exemplary leader. Prayer secures the leader against any form of temptation and serves as the glue that combines all the characteristics of leadership into the embodiment of a person to be a shining star.

Genesis 30:22
Then God remembered Rachel's plight and
answered her prayers by enabling her to have
children

17

PRAYER BRINGS REMEMBRANCE

Does God forget? This is a difficult question to answer but from scripture we see time and again that God remembered some-one for one thing or another. I believe the all-knowing God does not forget us but by the laws He has set in place we have to bring his word into action by our prayers. God will do nothing unless man prays.

Prayer is a legal permission for the sovereign God to move in the affairs of man. God has spoken to us through His word. It is up to us to enforce his word through prayer for us to see the manifestation of it. The ball is always in your court. You determine the set time of your remembrance. Scripture says, "Thou shalt arise and have mercy upon Zion; for the time to favour her, yea, the set time has come (Psalm 102:13)". Yes! God is ever ready to favour your cause and it takes prayer to cause him to arise.

God told Abraham it will take 400 years for his descendants to leave slavery but it took 430 years because at the set time their cries had not reached heaven until the 430th year before their cries reached God. Another instance was God telling Jeremiah that it will take 70 years for the nation to be in captivity. It took Daniel to understand the timing of God and he interceded for the entire nation of Israel to be freed from captivity. Yes, God has said it but your delay in prayer can delay its manifestation.

There are instances God decides to do something without your permission for His own purpose and plan. Elizabeth and Zachariah had given up on childbirth but God came in and Elizabeth conceived based on his own agenda. This is because he wanted their son John to be the forerunner for Jesus Christ. Your part is to pray and God will come in. If not today, it will be tomorrow but you must pray!

Jesus taught his disciples to pray for their daily bread. Prayer brings remembrance of the manifestation of God's daily benefits. Never forget that.

Isaiah 66:8

Who has heard such a thing? Who hath seen such things? Shall the earth be made to bring forth in one day? Or shall a nation be born at once? For as soon as Zion travailed, she brought forth her children.

18

PRAYER, THE LINK BETWEEN THE SPIRITUAL BLESSING AND THE PHYSICAL MANIFESTATION

Blessed be the God and Father of our Lord Jesus Christ, who has blessed us with every spiritual blessing in the heavenly places in Christ (Ephesians 1:3). Beloved, God has richly blessed us spiritually in Christ Jesus and these blessings would have to be manifested physically for all to witness who we are in Christ Je-sus. All spiritual blessings do not mean only physical possessions. They also include good health, peace, joy, long life, and all other good things.

The missing link between the spiritual blessing and we seeing it at work in our lives is prayer. Prayer will always bring into mani-festation every spiritual blessing. Many are the promises God has given us in the Bible but how many of us see it coming to pass in our lives? Those who give themselves to prayer will see it come to pass.

Before Jesus ascended to heaven, he told the disciples to wait (pray) for the Promise of the Father (Acts 1:4). The Promise, which is the Holy Spirit, was received by them because of their obedi-ence to wait.

Paul in his desire to see the church grow in the likeness of Jesus Christ said, "My little children, of whom I travail in birth again until Christ be formed in you (Galatians 4:19)". Christ in us is the hope of glory, Amen. The mystery of Christ in us will be evident

physically only by prayer. Christ in us is the same as the Holy Spirit in us. The Holy Spirit bears the fruit of love, joy, peace, patience, kindness, goodness, gentleness, faithfulness and self-control in our lives (Galatians 5:22). These characteristics will come out if we engage in prayer and allow the Holy Spirit to bear them in our lives. Prayer is always the machine that converts the spiritual to become physical.

All the promises of God have been fulfilled in Christ Jesus (2 Cor-inthians 1:20). This means every promise in the Bible with its con-ditions have been met by Jesus. You can then enjoy its benefits through prayer and faith in Christ Jesus.

Acts 4:31
And when they had prayed, the place where
they were assembled together was shaken;
and they were filled with the Holy Spirit, and
they spoke the word of God with boldness.

19

PRAYER BIRTHS POWER

Do you want to see the power of God at work in your life? Be-loved, it comes by prayer. Prayer births the power of God in your life. It is that power generated by the Spirit through prayer that gives utterance, manifestation and potency to the proclaimed word of God.

Jesus performed many miracles and they occurred between his prayers. As the scriptures recorded, "And in the morning, rising up a great while before day, he went out, and departed into a solitary place, and there prayed (Mark 11:35)." Jesus spent his early hours in prayer and at times he spent all night in prayers. Everyone was looking for Jesus but he made sure he had spent quality time in prayer before he attended to them. The strength and pow-er to meet the needs of all who sought him was as a result of his prayer life.

Now to Him who is able to do exceedingly abundantly above all that we ask or think, according to the power that works in us (Ephesians 3:20)… That Power in us comes alive by prayer.

The disciples were limited and did not know what to do when they were persecuted. They decided to resort to prayer and the place they assembled was shaken, at last they were filled with the Holy Spirit. The infilling of the Spirit was the power that gave them the boldness to preach and it all came by prayer.

1 Chronicles 4:10
And Jabez called on the God of Israel…

20

PRAYER BREAKS LIMITATIONS

In Christ Jesus there are no limits. Prayer breaks limitations, the mother of mediocrity. Every life God created has imbedded in it the power to grow and reproduce. The fall of man, man's own actions, and certain unknown factors retarded growth at point in time. But the good news is, by prayer the power and the grace of God breaks through any limitation.

Jesus had the opportunity to receive five loaves of bread and two fish from a young boy. Looking at the number of people who attended his conference, it was insignificant to be distributed to them for food. Five loaves of bread and two fish were limited but Jesus looked up to heaven and thanked God for them. He then broke the bread and distributed it to the people.

Scripture says they ate as much as they wanted and there were twelve baskets full of left overs. What an amazing God we serve! By prayer what seems to be of a limitation became a blessing and an overflow. The limitation on the bread was broken as Jesus blessed and thanked God for it.

I don't know what you have in your hands right now but if you will take it to God in prayer and understand how to operate with what is in your hands, beloved, you will experience multiplication and growth.

The abundance of God always amazes me. Everything God created is always in abundance and it's forever. God created the sun and the sun is there forever. He created the air, plants, and every-thing we see around us.

All things were made by him; and without him was not anything made that was made (John 1:3). He created all things for his pleasure. There has never been a time the experts have said the sea was running dry or oxygen was running out. He is a God of abun-dance. He loves increase and progress.

That is why He told Adam and Eve to multiply and be fruitful. Our God is a God of multiplication. He is a great business man. He gave only His begotten son and now He has millions of sons all over the world. What an amazing God we serve!

Jabez was a man who analysed his life and realised he was limited. All he did was to call on the God of Israel, saying, "oh that you would bless me and enlarge my border, and that your hand might be with me, and that you would keep me from harm so that it might not bring me pain! And God granted what he asked (1 Chronicles 4:10)." Beloved, God is ready to grant you your request of increase, progress, development, growth, expansion, etc., just call on him now!

You have hired enough experts and the business is still where it is. Have you resorted to God and the leading of His Holy Spirit? Without the help of the Holy Spirit you will be limited. Any Chris-tian who gets the best results in any endeavour can be attributed to the help of the Holy Spirit. You need him now like never before. Call on Him now and He will help you.

He will move the barriers and obstacles hindering your progress in life and destiny. He will tell you of the future and the right step to take so your business does not become obsolete. Until you decide to fellowship with him or pray to Him then your breakthrough will be limited.

Beloved, nothing can stand against the power of God. It does not matter the demonic forces against you. They are already in the past because Jesus has defeated them. Enforce your victory through prayer and see the power of God at work in your life. You are blessed!

John 17:15

I do not pray that you should take them out
of the world, but that you should keep them
from the evil one.

21

PRAYER SECURES THE FUTURE

Today is yesterday's tomorrow. Tomorrow will come by the grace of God just as you are in today. What are you expect-ing the Lord to do for you tomorrow? Secure tomorrow by your prayers today. For tomorrow's harvest is dependent on the seed you sow today. Prayer serves as the seed that sprouts tomorrow when planted today. The joy of any believer tomorrow is depen-dant on the sacrifice of their prayers today. Secure the future now beloved with your prayers today.

Jesus prayed into the future of what he anticipated might happen. He knew that the enemy could frustrate the destiny of those who believed in him and so he prayed for the Father to keep them from the evil one (John 17:15). Beloved, what are your expectations for tomorrow? What do you desire to see in your life, business, career, family, church and nation? Committing the future in the hands of God is the best decision to make. Teaching his disciples how to pray, he taught them to pray for the Lord to lead them not into temptation but to deliver them from evil (Matthew 6:13). This is a prayer that secures the future.

Jesus said, "the seed is the word of God (Luke 8:11)". The word of God engaged in prayer sows seeds into your future. This means when you reach your future those prayers will be speaking for you. For instance, if you are a young person you can declare –

"with long life the Lord will satisfy me" (Psalm 91:16). What this means is you are sowing seeds of long life into your future and nothing and I mean nothing, can cut short your life because this prayer will be fighting to secure your destiny.

He is the Alpha and the Omega, the beginning and the end, the first and the last. The Lord knows the end from the beginning. He is the one who teaches you what is best for you, guides you along the best pathway for your life, advises and watches over you (Isa-iah 48:17, Psalm 32:8). He knows the future better than you do and he is the same yesterday, today and forever (Hebrews 13:8).

So he says trust in him with all your heart and lean not on your own understanding (Proverbs 3:5). The Lord is far capable of exceeding your expectations for the future. It will be good for you to commit your expectations of the future to him. For he is able to keep that which we commit into his hands (2 Timothy 1:12). For in his hands He is far able to deliver, keep, nurture, grow, preserve, beautify, establish, expand, sanctify and prosper. The one who prays about the future is confident of tomorrow.

Evangelist R.A. Torrey said on prayer: The reason why many fail in battle is because they wait until the hour of battle. The reason why others succeed is because they have gained their victory on their knees long before the battle came ... Anticipate your battles; fight them on your knees before temptation comes, and you will always have victory.

Ephesians 6:12

For we do not wrestle against flesh and
blood, but against principalities, against
powers, against the rulers of the darkness of
this age, against spiritual hosts of wickedness
in the heavenly places.

22

PRAYER IS A WEAPON FOR WARFARE

The devil is against every human being including those working for him. He is roaming about like an angry lion seeking someone to devour. The book of Revelation says woe to you inhabitants of the earth because the devil is come down to you (Revelation 12:12). He sometimes influences people to fight and resist your progress in life. That is why our fight is not against flesh and blood. The Christian is admonished to fight the good fight of faith (1 Timothy 6:12) and behind every battle is strategy. Your strategy is to pray with the right scriptures and trust God to do the battle on your behalf. Victory does not come by magic. Map up deliberate prayer tactics by searching for the right scriptures to use in prayer. The warrior in you is coming alive!

The purpose of the enemy is to steal, kill and destroy (John 10:10). There is no need to fight the wrong enemy. If there is an evidence of the purpose of the devil in any situation then it calls for battle. Jesus said I came that you might have life and have it more abun-dantly (John 10:10). Any resistance to the abundant life Jesus offers is from the devil. Resist him and he will flee from you (James 4:7).

Jesus is Lord over everything and there is no place for the devil. Trust in God to come out victorious in any condition. What the devil does is to distract and kill your faith. Get rid of any distractions and focus your mind on Him. Our God is good, faithful, mighty and merciful. Let God fight for you through your prayers and find your rest in him because he has won the victory for you.

Proverbs 21:1
The king's heart is in the hand of the Lord,
Like the rivers of water;
He turns it wherever He wishes.

23

PRAYER CHANGES PEOPLE AND SITUATIONS

There is so much power in the life of an individual. When that power is channeled towards evil it becomes havoc for the rest of mankind. Remember people like Saddam Hussein, Adolf Hitlar, Idi Amin, Osama Bin Laden, etc. These were individuals whose actions affected hundreds of thousands of people. We can-not underestimate the power of one. It took one man Adam for sin and death to enter the world and it took one man Jesus to bring salvation to all of mankind.

If an individual is not heading towards the right course, it calls for alarm. You don't need to relax and say this will not result in anything. If your action can influence the person to do what is right, it is important to do so but whereby you cannot get in touch with such a person, prayer can reach him or her. Even if you have an opportunity to speak to such a person you need to add prayer. This is because at times their actions are influenced by unseen forces that no amount of human words will yield any result in their lives except the words spoken to God through prayers.

The king's heart is in the hand of the Lord, like the rivers of water; He turns it wherever He wishes (Proverbs 21:1). It will be better to pray for that person than to complain and insult him or her. The king's heart or the president's heart is in the hand of the Lord. Your parents, managers, pastors, judges, etc., have their hearts in the hands of the Lord. Prayer is a tool to cause God to change their hearts on any matter.

The children of Israel by a decree of one man were to be annihilated but by their prayer and fasting the verdict went in their favour (Esther 3:9). God can do anything through you for his glory. Don't sit down and watch events pass you by. Your prayers can change things or the course of history to the glory of God.

Jesus prayed for Peter for his faith not to fail because the enemy has asked to sift him like wheat (Luke 22:32). The enemy today might be sifting the lives of certain people. It is for us to pray for them and not to complaint or insult them. The only thing that will change them is your prayer. Indeed, prayer changes people.

Proverbs 24:10
If you faint in the day of adversity,
Your strength is small.

24

PRAYER AFFIRMS THE VICTORY

Through death Jesus destroyed he who had the power of death that is the devil and delivered all those who through fear of death were all of their lifetime subject to bondage (Hebrews 2:14-15). The death and resurrection of our Lord Jesus Christ has set us free from the bondage of death. Death here also means sickness, poverty, weakness, defeat and any bad thing in this world. Often people are in fear of dying because of one thing or another but be-loved you are free from the bondage of death. You will live abundantly and declare the works of the Lord.

Prayer affirms the victory Jesus has won for us. Jesus disarmed the spiritual rulers and authorities and shamed them publicly by his victory over them on the cross (Colossians 2:14-15). We pray out of the position and mindset of victory because of what Jesus has done for us. Scripture says, "The path of the just is as the shining light, that shineth more and more unto the perfect day (Proverbs 4:20)." You are the just (righteous) of the Lord and your path is to shine brighter and brighter each day. Prayer affirms that bright-ness because that is who we are. Our light has come and we only need to arise and shine.

Christians are victorious people. We must continually abide in the word and on the prayer altar in order to keep building spiritual strength for the day of battle and to preserve God's blessings in our lives. For if you faint in the day of adversity then your strength is small (Proverbs 24:10).

Romans 14:17

For the kingdom of God is not meat and drink; but righteousness, and peace, and joy in the Holy Ghost.

25

PRAYER UNITES WITH GOD'S PURPOSES

When prayer meets God's purposes, the physical manifesta-tion is irrefutable. God's purposes are outlined in the Bible.

His purpose is also his will for us. His ultimate plan is to establish his kingdom here on earth. This kingdom is a spiritual kingdom of righteousness, peace and joy (Romans 14:17).

From that time Jesus began to preach, and to say, Repent: for the kingdom of heaven is at hand (Matthew 4:17). Jesus' desire for the household of Israel was to repent, that is to have a change of mind from expecting a physical kingdom to that of a spiritual kingdom that comes by faith and not the law.

Now, our prayers can establish the kingdom of God in our lives, families, churches and nations. Everywhere you desire to see the kingdom of God gaining expression will be possible through your prayers. Your prayers can establish the righteousness, peace and joy of God in any area and over every situation.

It is God's plan that righteousness would reign in his Kingdom. Righteousness is having a right standing with God. It is a free gift given to you when you believe in Jesus Christ (2 Corinthians 5:21). Righteousness results in exaltation (Proverbs 14:34), it brings de-liverance from death (Psalm 34:19), flourishing (Psalm 72:7), ex-cellence (Proverbs 12:26), favour (Proverbs 14:9) and many other benefits. The peace and joy of God comes by the fruit of the Holy

Spirit that is at work in the life of the believer. It is the responsibil-ity of believers to allow the kingdom of God in them (righteous-ness, peace and joy) to gain expression through them to affect their households, communities and all those they come in contact with. God desires his kingdom to spread to the ends of the earth and from generation to generation.

This can be made possible through our prayers. We must pray for righteousness, peace and joy to fill the homes of people, commu-nities, churches, schools, and the nations of the world. As we do this the kingdom of God will fill all the earth.

Proverbs 15:8

The sacrifice of the wicked is an
abomination to the Lord, But the prayer of
the upright is His delight.

26

PRAYER HONOURS GOD

The prayer of a righteous man honours God. The law of prayer has been set in place by God and we honour Him when we live it. It delights the heart of God to see righteous people offer up prayers. When God is honoured He shows up with his manifest presence. We can see that during the dedication of the temple of Solomon (2 Chronicles 5:14).

Every righteous man who prays carries the presence of God with him wherever he goes. His speech and actions are directed by the presence of God and so brings honour to God in all he does. When God is honoured, he shows up to the defence of the righteous. When the three Hebrew boys were cast in the fiery furnace, God showed up as the fourth man. The fire did not harm them nor did any smell of fire come upon them (Daniel 3).

God is our Father and just as every Father delights to see his children do well in life so does our Father. Jesus said, "And in that day you will ask Me nothing. Most assuredly, I say to you, whatever you ask the Father in My name He will give you. Until now you have asked nothing in My name. Ask, and you will receive, that your joy may be full (John 16:23-24)." God wants to see you joyful and happy in life. When you ask in accordance to his will and purposes he provides and that brings him honour. When people ask you how were you able to achieve that thing and you tell them it's because of the grace of God, it brings honour to God.

Acts 1:4

And being assembled together with them, He commanded them not to depart from Jerusalem, but to wait for the Promise of the Father, "which," He said, "you have heard from Me;

27

PRAYER ORIGINATES AND SHAPES GREAT MOVEMENTS OF GOD

Every great movement of God is preceded by prayer. Prayer births, shapes, outlines and gives meaning to such a move-ment. The massive outpouring of the Holy Spirit in the nations of the world would happen only through our prayers. Historical revival movements of God happened because of prayer. Men and women decided to pray, fast and wait upon God to manifest his presence to save and deliver dying souls.

Missionary work without prayer and much prayer will be an exercise with less impact. The work of the missionary is to save and raise men of prayer. Prayer serves as the highway that missionaries ride on to preach the gospel. The missionary must spend much time in prayer and prayer must take much of his time. This is because the power that comes from the gospel is felt from the ut-terance of a prayerful man.

Before His ascension, Jesus told the disciples to "wait" (pray) for the promise of the Father. This great movement that is taking over the world begun by prayer. Prayer originated this movement and nurtured it from being destroyed by wicked and carnal men.

When the disciples were being attacked and threatened by the au-thorities of their days, they assembled together and prayed (Acts 4:31).

Paul often times requested the church to pray for him or what he was beginning would have easily been destroyed by wicked men who have no faith (2Thessalonians 3:1-2).

We cannot underestimate the potency of prayer in evangelism. Prayer is the bedrock, backbone, pillar, anchor and support for missionary work.

2 Chronicles 7:14

If My people who are called by My name will humble themselves, and pray and seek My face, and turn from their wicked ways, then I will hear from heaven, and will forgive their sin and heal their land

28

PRAYER INFLUENCES GOD

Your prayer affects God and God's conduct is influenced by prayer. Your faith in Jesus and prayer will always move God in your direction but cries and self-pity will never get the attention of heaven. God's desire is for his children to humble themselves, pray and repent of their wicked ways. He is always ready to help us only if we humble ourselves and pray.

King Hezekiah was told by the prophet that he was going to die but he influenced God by his prayer and lived an additional 15 more years. No situation is permanent. Your prayers can turn things around in your favour. You may be a young lady desiring marriage, your prayers can influence God to bring the right man into your life.

Don't give up, God is never too late or unfaithful. He is still God and He changes not. Sarah was 90 years old before giving birth. Don't throw in the towel, the battle is to your favour. It is a good battle because the end has already been declared that you are the winner.

Don't spoil your testimony. You are never wiser than God to tell him when to act for you or else you will stop serving him. In fact, when you stop serving him He is still God and that will not change anything about him. His thoughts are different from yours but al-ways know the plans he has for you are of good and not of evil, to give you a future and a hope (Jeremiah 29:11).

Jesus never gave up on God. In fact, when things became very hard for him he prayed that God would take the cup of suffering from him and yet in his prayers he said, "yet not my will, but yours be done (Luke 22:42)." He wanted to influence God through his prayers and yet in the same prayers he gave God the go-ahead that it might be fulfilled of the scriptures.

Beloved, it is my prayer that you will never come to a point of giv-ing up in life. Life in itself is not fair but the opportunity to pray is fair for all. Rise up from where you are and go back to your Father in prayers. He is always ready to hear your prayers. No amount of sin can block your access to him. In fact, he said he will be mer-ciful to your unrighteousness, and your sins and lawless deeds he will remember no more (Hebrews 8:12).

In Luke 15 Jesus gave three parables and they were the parables of the lost sheep, the lost coin and the lost son. When the sheep got lost the owner went in search for it and when the coin got lost the owner swept the house in search for it but when the son got lost the father didn't go in search for him. Why did the father not go in search for the lost son?

It is because the father knows the son has in him the ability to know he is lost and work his way back home. Beloved, all I am trying to say is you are a man or woman with the ability to come to God from where you have fallen short. He will not cast you out nor condemn you. Your prayers can influence him now and forev-er more. He still loves you.

Isaiah 53:1
Who has believed our report? And to whom
has the arm of the Lord been revealed?

29

PRAYER EXALTS GOD'S POWER

Who said your God is not powerful? And who is he who is mocking at your God? The power of our God cannot be fathomed by any human mind. Our God is so powerful than the word powerful itself. A time came when the king of Assyria and his officers mocked Hezekiah and the God of Israel with insults upon insults. The king of Assyria said "…what makes you think your God can rescue you from me?" (2 Chronicles 32:14). I don't know who or what has been mocking your God but be rest as-sured that God will come to your rescue and your enemies will be put to shame if you will pray.

Scripture goes on to say that King Hezekiah and the prophet Isaiah son of Amos cried out in prayer to God in heaven and the Lord sent an angel who destroyed the Assyrian army with all its commanders and officers. In fact, the Assyrian king Sennacherib was forced to return home in disgrace and some of his own sons killed him there with a sword (2 Chronicles 32:20-21). Your prayer will exalt the power of God on your behalf.

The Israelites would have been destroyed if the King and the Prophet had not interceded for them. All that God is waiting for is your prayers concerning that issue and you will see his power at work. If God is powerful, why doesn't he take away all the evil in the world now? Beloved, God is all powerful but he cannot defile his own rule to intervene on earth without the permission of man.

He has given man the legal rights to allow Him on earth in case we need him and prayer is what makes that possible (Genesis 1:28, Psalm 115:16, Matthew 18:18).

Never give up on prayer. It will exalt the power of God on your behalf. Jesus said to his disciples that he could ask the Father and he will send more than twelve legions of angels to his rescue (Mat-thew 26:53). Jesus' Father is now your Father. Ask him whatsoever you desire according to his will and he will prove himself strong on your behalf.

1 Kings 18:24

Then you call on the name of your gods, and I
will call on the name of the Lord; and the God
who answers by fire, He is God.

30

PRAYER ACKNOWLEDGES GOD'S BEING

One wise man said if there is a man to pray then there's a God to answer. It is sad to say in today's world a number of peo-ple don't believe in the existence of God, yet God has manifested himself in the things he has created around us. Satan, the god of this world, has blindfolded their minds that they are unable to see the glorious light of Jesus Christ through the gospel (2 Corinthians 4:4). Prayer helps to remove the blindfolding of the devil for all to see and acknowledge Jesus as their LORD and personal saviour.

Answered prayer proves to the world the existence of our God. The spiritual world is even more real than the physical world be-cause the physical came out of the spiritual yet people refuse the existence of the spiritual world.

Elijah had to prove to the worshippers of Baal that the God we serve is alive and powerful. He called for a contest on Mount Car-mel between the prophets of Baal and himself. He made them arrange an altar with pieces of bull on it and said the God who answers by setting fire to the wood is the true God. The prophets of Baal did all they could but their god never answered them but the God of Elijah answered by setting fire to the altar of Elijah (1 Kings 18).

At the tomb of Lazarus, Jesus prayed by thanking God for hearing him and to prove that He was sent by God. Jesus is God in the flesh and he made people acknowledge who He is by prayer (John 11:40-44).

Our God is still a prayer answering God. He never changes. He is the same yesterday, today and forever. Prove His worth by your prayer today.

Psalm 103:1
Bless the Lord, O my soul;
And all that is within me, bless
His holy name!

31

PRAYER ADORES GOD'S PROVIDENCE

The prayer of praise, worship and thanksgiving adores God's providence. Merriam-Webster dictionary defines providence as God conceived; as the power sustaining and guiding human destiny. Aside our offerings to God, we can also honour him with the fruit of our lips through praise, worship and thanksgiving.

When Jesus taught the disciples how to pray, he began by saying "Our Father who art in heaven hallowed be thy name" (Mathew 6:9). Prayer gives the opportunity to hallow the name of the Lord.

I like the way the Psalmist said it:

> Bless the Lord, O my soul;
> And all that is within me, bless His holy name!
> Bless the Lord, O my soul,
> And forget not all His benefits:
> Who forgives all your iniquities,
> Who heals all your diseases,
> Who redeems your life from destruction,
> Who crowns you with lovingkindness and tender mercies,
> Who satisfies your mouth with good things,
> So that your youth is renewed like the eagle's.

There are so many things to be thankful for than to complain about. Adore His providence today and see his glory at work in your life.

At times, God ties His blessings to our praise. The Psalmist said "Let the people praise You, O God; Let all the people praise You. Then the earth shall yield her increase; God, our own God, shall bless us. God shall bless us, And all the ends of the earth shall fear Him" (Psalm 67:5-7). Don't miss out on this opportunity. Bless the Lord at all times and even when you find yourself in a difficult situation, your praise will put you in a position to receive from His treasures.

Let me open your understanding to something remarkable here. The scripture says "Bless the Lord, O my soul; And all that is with-in me, bless His holy name!" Do you know you are made of dust and that there is oil in you? Do you know there is gold, diamond, copper, aluminium, and all the minerals you find under the sand in you now? Do you know you have your children, grandchildren, business, ministry and all your dreams in you? In case you didn't know let me put it to you that they are in you. You are no ordinary person.

Therefore, as you bless the Lord with everything in you what you are saying is, God, apart from the heart, the liver, kidney, small and big intestines, the colon, blood, water, etc., in my body, I bless you also with Christ in me or your Holy Spirit in me and all the minerals and dreams I have in me. When you thank and praise God this way, your increase has no option than to burst out.

I remember a time when I went to church with headache and as I worshipped I declared to the Lord that everything in me including what is in my head should bless the Lord. After the worship I real-ised the headache was gone. You know why? God always perfects that which we hand over to him so keep on blessing him. God is for you beloved. Adore His providence through your prayer of praise, worship and thanksgiving.

Jude 20
But you, beloved, building yourselves up on
your most holy faith, praying in
the Holy Spirit.

32

PRAYER EMBOLDENS YOU

Boldness, the first qualification of a leader is very relevant for your success in life. Boldness distinguishes a leader from a follower. It elevates the lowly and causes him to be noticed. It sets the pace between the winner and the loser. It causes one to access and dare great things that an ordinary person will never do. It frightens the enemy and makes magnificent barriers appear insignificant. No wonder the Lion is noted as the king of the jungle because of its boldness and the righteous is likened to the Lion in boldness. Prayer can embolden you to your position of glorification.

Jesus was noticed for his boldness (John 7:26) and I believe His prayer life made him bold. When the disciples were afraid of the threats and persecutions, their only prayer was for God to grant them boldness to speak His word (Acts 4:13). And when they had prayed, the place where they were assembled together was shak-en; and they were all filled with the Holy Spirit, and they spoke the word of God with boldness (Acts 4:31).

Paul told the church of Ephesus to pray for him that utterance may be given to him, that he may open his mouth boldly to make known the mystery of the gospel (Ephesians 6:19). The gospel accompanied with boldness of speech that emanates from prayer brings about tremendous results.

God told Joshua over and over again to be strong and courageous (Joshua 1:6-8). Beloved, life requires boldness. We are not wres-tling with flesh and blood. Every new level has its own challenges but the Lord is with you, only be strong and courageous. Praying in the language of the Spirit has the ability to embolden you for any assignment. Whether you are scheduled for an interview or you have an examination to write or even a presentation to make, prayer makes boldness available.

Romans 10:10
…with the mouth confession is made unto salvation

33

PRAYER BRINGS SALVATION

Salvation comes from the Greek word *'soteria'* which connotes deliverance, healing, protection redemption and freedom from all evil. Anything in this world that is contrary to what salvation brings calls for prayer. Prayer has the power to usher in the sal-vation of God into an unsaved life and extend that same salvation into issues that are contrary to us.

Until one opens the mouth, he stands not the chance of enjoying the benefits of salvation. Prayer brings about salvation. Anyone who calls on the Lord shall be saved (Acts 2:21). For it is by believing in your heart that you are made right with God and it is by confession with your mouth that you are saved (Romans 10:9-10). As long as we find ourselves on earth and in our human bodies, we will face situations, obstacles and limitations. It takes courage, faith and confession that brings salvation to overcome.

Scripture talks about Jesus witnessing the good confession before Pontius Pilate (2 Timothy 6:13). This fight of faith we are into has to do with our confession. We having the same spirit of faith, as it is written, I believed, and therefore have I spoken; we also believe, and therefore speak (2 Corinthians 4:13). If you believe in God's salvation then declare his word over that contrary situation. It is important not to consider the contrary evidence at the moment nor waver through unbelief. Scripture spoke of Abraham that who against hope believed in hope and he staggered not at the promise of God through unbelief, but was strong in faith, giving glory to God. That is a good way to fight a good fight of faith.

When the devil tempted Jesus, he was already full of the Holy Spirit and so he was able to overcome the devil through the scrip-tures he spoke from his Spirit (Luke 4:1-13). I remember what my spiritual father shared with the church, that if you want a partic-ular scripture to tackle a certain problem, pray in the Spirit and the Holy Spirit will bring out a particular scripture and when you speak that word it will be full of power. A Spirit filled declaration always overcomes.

Isaiah 60:1
Arise, shine; For your light has come!
And the glory of the LORD is risen upon you.

34

PRAYER OPENS UP YOUR DESTINY

Merriam-Webster online dictionary defines destiny as what happens in the future: the things that someone or something will experience in the future. God has purposed that it will end up well with each and every one of his righteous children (Psalm 37:37). This is God's intent for you as his righteous son or daughter. Anything contrary to what God's word says about you and your future calls for prayer.

Prophet Jeremiah prophesied that the Israelites will be in captivity for 70 years (Jeremiah 29:10). The fact that they will be in captivity for 70 years does not mean it came to an end by chance. Daniel had to fast and pray to enforce the prophetic word spoken by the Prophet Jeremiah (Daniel 9:1-2). Beloved, the enemy will always try to keep you in captivity or in bondage of one thing or another. He does not want your future to be peaceful and great. That is why you need to resist him by submitting yourself to God and His Word (James 4:7).

God told Abraham that his seed will be in captivity for 400 years. The destiny of the Israelites was in slavery until their cries reached God (Exodus 3:7). Isaac entreated God for his wife to open up her womb to be fruitful (Genesis 25:21). Jabez's destiny was bleak un-til he prayed (1 Corinthians 4:10). The Israelites destiny was in captivity until Daniel prayed (Daniel 10:12). Jesus' destiny was in serious contention until he spent time in prayer at Gethsemane for

God's will to be done (Matthew 26:39). When Jesus was being bap-tised and praying, the heaven was opened (Luke 3:21). The dis-ciples were being intimidated and hindered in their assignment until they met together in prayer again (Acts 4:31).

I don't know what is trying to shield your shine in business, family or personal life but you can arise by prayer and shine for your light has come and the glory of the Lord is risen upon you. Prayer carries with it the capacity to open up your destiny for you to be celebrated here on earth.

Luke 3:21-22

Now when all the people were baptised, it came to pass, that Jesus also being baptised, and praying, the heaven was opened, And the Holy Ghost descended in a bodily shape like a dove upon him, and a voice came from heaven, which said, Thou art my beloved Son;

in thee I am well pleased.

35

PRAYER BRINGS THE ANOINTING

One wonderful thing prayer brings from God upon the min-istry and an individual's life is an indescribable and unique thing called the anointing. In prayer, we can obtain the anointing that makes God's truth powerful, attract, draw, edify, convict and save lives.

The anointing is what everyone needs for distinction in ministry, business, education, government and life in general. To anoint is to put oil on, where the oil represents the Holy Spirit. When God's oil comes upon your life, it brings about speed, preservation, heal-ing, fruitfulness, power to do the impossible, distinction, qualifi-cation for God's work among many others. The anointing in itself is priceless and beyond measure. Man cannot give it to you. It only comes from God and it is through prayer.

E. M. Bounds said, "it is the anointing that gives the words of the preacher such power, sharpness and point and that creates such brokenness of heart, convict the conscience in many a dead congregation. The anointing is what distinguishes and separates preaching from all human speeches, lectures and presentations. The word of God that is embedded in the anointing is what saves and brings healing and deliverance to many. It is not about shout-ing in preaching that shows the word is powerful. It is the word that proceeds from a prayerful preacher that makes the difference. All the energy of God supports and impregnates revealed truth."

When Jesus was baptised and praying, the Holy Spirit descended on Him like a dove and that was the anointing that came upon Jesus for ministry. Set your heart today to seek the unction through prayer and enjoy an unending benefit from the awesomeness of God. When the disciples were having difficulty casting out the devil in the young boy, Jesus said such kind cannot go unless by prayer (Mark 9:29). Prayer produces that unction or anointing that makes difficult or impossible situations possible.

Before Jesus released the disciples, he told them to wait (pray) for the promise of the Father. The promise was the power or anoint-ing of the Holy Ghost to help them in ministry. We cannot delude ourselves in thinking we can do the works the apostles did with-out prayer and the anointing. Prayer indeed brings the anointing.

Ephesians 5:16
...redeeming the time, because the days are evil.

36

PRAYER COMPRESSES AND REDEEMS TIME

To redeem is basically to buy back and prayer is one of the means to buy back time. Time as we know is perishable, neu-tral, priceless, treasure, transient, currency of life, etc. The tran-sient nature of time is that it is fleeting and does not come back again. There is no way you can renew time. It is a non-renewable resource. Once you spend it, you cannot get it back. So how does prayer buy back time since you cannot reverse time?

The truth is prayer engages the God who created time to step in your affairs to compress time for you to redeem it. What this means is the time you should have spent to achieve something that you wasted, God is able to give you the grace to pursue that same thing and achieve in less time.

For instance, here is Jesus and his mother Mary at a wedding cele-bration. The wine they were serving the guests got finished. Mary then tells the servants at the wedding that "whatever he says to you do it". So Jesus instructed them to fill the water pots with wa-ter and they were very smart to fill the pots to the brim and he told them to draw some out and take to the master of the feast. When he tasted, it was wine. Hallelujah!

Now watch something here:

1. Shortage of wine means the demand was more than what

was available.

2. More wine for the feast will mean more time to go in search of wine to buy.

3. If they were to prepare a new wine it would have taken them many days to have it realised.

4. Mary calling on Jesus to help was a form of intercession.

5. Jesus instructing the servants was like the servants spending time with God and knowing what to do.

6. The miracle of water turning into wine was God's way of compressing time to redeem the time to prepare or go in search for wine.

God is able to restore the time you wasted yesterday. He is the re-storer of waste places. Once you engage him in studies, business, ministry, etc., he is far able to compress and redeem the time for you. It can take you about a week to understand a given subject but when God steps in it can take you an hour.

In case you wasted your youthful life, God is able to renew your strength and cause you to enjoy abundant life. Engage God today and he will help you accomplish things that in reality have to take many years to achieve in less time.

Paul told the church to redeem the time because the days are evil (Ephesians 5:16). Prayer will help you maximise the opportunities of today because the Lord will guide you along the best pathway for your life so you don't waste time. He will also advise and watch over you. You get all these benefits in the secret place of prayer.

Isaiah 62:6-7

I have set watchmen on your walls,
O Jerusalem; They shall never hold
their peace day or night.
You who make mention of the Lord, do not
keep silent, And give Him no rest till He
establishes And till He makes Jerusalem a
praise in the earth.

37

PRAYER MAKES YOU A
PRAISE ON EARTH

To be a praise on earth is to be admired by everyone. Ev-ery colourful destiny attracts attention. Prayer puts you in a position to be admired by everyone. There was a leper who came to Jesus and worshipped him, saying, Lord if you are willing you can heal me and make me clean (Matthew 8:2). This was a man who was disgraced by the disease of leprosy.

Scripture did not mention how old he was but said he was a man. This also connotes that he was likely to have a family or a voca-tion. In those times there was no cure for leprosy so if anyone had the disease, he was quarantined from the people or community.

Imagine, if he was the bread winner of the family, everything will start working against the family from the day he was noted to be a leper. He could not go to work anymore, he could not spend time with the family or even be at the synagogue to hear the teachers of the law. Shame, disgrace and poverty would have accompanied this man all the days of his life.

But thanks be unto God, this man met Jesus. Jesus reached out his hand and touched him, saying, I am willing be healed and in-stantly the leprosy disappeared (Matthew 8:3). Now this man can now go back to his family, vocation, and synagogue. He can freely move among people without any limitation.

This man calling on Jesus was an act of prayer. I believe when Jesus was on the mountain preaching he hid somewhere among the rocks and he heard Jesus saying, "Everyone who asks, receives… If you sinful people know how to give good gifts to your children, how much more will your heavenly Father give good gifts to those who ask him" (Matthew 7:8, 11). He therefore asked Jesus to heal him but was not sure if Jesus was willing. Beloved, Jesus is willing any day, anytime, anywhere to meet your need. The response he received from Jesus made him a praise on earth. You can also call on God to change any worse situation for it to result in praise to His glory.

Genesis 27:28-29

Therefore may God give you of the dew of
heaven, of the fatness of the earth, and plenty of
grain and wine.
Let people serve you, and nations bow down
to you. Be master over your brethren, and let
your mother's sons bow down to you. Cursed
be everyone who curses you, and blessed be
those who bless you!"

38

PRAYER SERVES AS AN INHERITANCE

Merriam-Webster dictionary says Inheritance is money, prop-erty etc., that is received from someone when that person dies. Inheritance also means the act of inheriting something. And to inherit is to receive (property, a right, title, etc.) by succession or under a will. Within this context I will define inheritance to mean, to receive a blessing by prayer from someone, particularly parents before their immediate transition from earth.

The dictionary said inheritance can be money, property, etc., meaning it can include a prayer blessing. There are many examples in the Bible for us to learn from and one of them is the story of Jacob and Esau.

Before their father Isaac died he requested for venison from the elder brother Esau who by Jewish tradition is the rightful successor of the father before he hands over the inheritance he has for him. I would like you to note something here: The inheritance Jacob and Esau received from their father Isaac was an inheritance of prayer.

Nowhere does the bible record that Isaac divided the cattle, goats, sheep and land among his sons but rather he gave them his blessing. Jacob had to ran away from his brother Esau because he deceived him for the inheritance of prayer blessings which was due Esau. Jacob ran away with only a staff but because of the spiritual inheritance delivered by prayer he returned with two companies

(Genesis 32:10).

In Genesis 49 before Jacob was gathered to his people, he called his children and delivered the prayer of inheritance unto them.

David prayed for Solomon before he left the scene and when Solomon ascended the throne those prayers began to answer to him (Psalm 72). As part of the prayer he said "and to him shall be given the gold of Sheba" This prayer of inheritance located Queen Sheba and brought her to Jerusalem to hand over the gold of She-ba to King Solomon (1Kings 10:10).

Jesus left us an inheritance through prayer that we may be one, kept from the evil one, sanctified by the truth, his love may be in us and Him in us (John 17). Parents should not underestimate this wisdom lesson of prayer as serving as an inheritance. This will be a greater blessing to the next generation than mere houses, money and cars.

Jeremiah 33:3
Call to Me and I will answer you, and show you
great and mighty things, which
you do not know.

39

PRAYER CONNECTS WITH DIVINITY

Prayer is the only vehicle that connects earth to heaven. It is the only medium through which God gets the opportunity to display his power on earth. Once we call on him in the name of Jesus, he hears us and answers us. God has the solution for all of life's problems. The wisdom, knowledge, understanding, intelligence for solving difficult problems are from God.

The mobile phone makes it possible to talk to anyone anywhere in the world as long as you dial in the right numbers and your con-tacts are in a coverage zone. It is so amazing how this technology works.

Dialling in the right numbers to connect to God is basically calling on God in accordance with His word which contains His will and purpose. As long as your call is based on the word of God, you will find God in a coverage area and He will answer to you. His answer is what you need to be on top of situations and circum-stances in your life. His answer is what can lift you from nobody to somebody. His answer is what will distinguish your life and destiny from the majority. His answer is what will deliver and honour you in that difficult situation. His answer is all you need to have all your needs met.

Call on him now and the President of the entire universe is ready to have discussions with you. You need not book an appointment.

He is always there for you. You are so precious to him. The one who has the solution in life and in the entire world is always there for you 24/7. Why the need to worry or be anxious? He is waiting on you to call. He has many things to show you. Call on Him now!

Jesus' secret was as a result of his connection with God. Between His prayer times were the miracles and great sermons. His connection with the Father was so strong that when He was made sin for us He said, "my God my God why have you forsaken me" (Matthew 27:46). Jesus said of His own he can do nothing and as he hears he judges (John 5:30). He was ready to hear from God any day, anytime and anywhere. He was so sensitive to God.

Prayer does not always have to be with shouts and utterances. At times prayer simply has to come from your heart (i.e. your spirit or inner man) and God who knows your heart and what the Spirit is saying will answer you (Romans 8:26-27). I believe Jesus walked in this realm of revelation about prayer also and enjoyed the ben-efit of receiving from God to judge any situation.

Be connected to God now!

Acts 1:14

These all continued in one accord in prayer
and supplication, with the women, and Mary
the Mother of Jesus, and with his brethren.

40

PRAYER IS FOR EVERYONE

Every Christian must take up the responsibility of prayer. It is for everyone and not some small majority of people they call prayer force. If one shall chase a thousand and two shall put ten thousand to flight (Deuteronomy 32:30), then I don't know how many will be chased away if all believers come together with one accord in prayer.

Individual prayer life is very vital and so is collective prayer. Everywhere prayer is needed it's a call to duty and exemption is not a better option. Jesus taught the disciples how to pray in order for each one of them to take up responsibility when it comes to prayer. The 'pray for me' syndrome is too much in the church now. People find every excuse not to pray but they seldom find an excuse to pray. That is why the church is weak and power seem to be lacking because men and women are failing to pray.

The power of one man cannot be underestimated when it comes to prayer. God used one man Moses, to bring deliverance to the nation of Israel and God used one man, Jesus to bring salva-tion to us all. You are that man whose prayers God can use to save your family, to heal the sick, to raise the dead, to bring his kingdom into governments, schools, nations, etc.

You must arise and take responsibility when it comes to prayer because prayer is for every believer.

GOD BLESS YOU.

www.ingramcontent.com/pod-product-compliance
Lightning Source LLC
Chambersburg PA
CBHW051426150726
48000CB00005B/1971